CEOLFRITH VICTORIAN POETS
SAMUEL LAYCOCK

SAMUEL LAYCOCK

SELECTED POEMS

EDITED WITH
AN INTRODUCTION BY
GLYN HUGHES

CEOLFRITH PRESS
SUNDERLAND
1981

CEOLFRITH PRESS

Samuel Laycock — Selected Poems
Introduction and selection © 1981 Glyn Hughes

First edition November 1981 Ceolfrith 66
First printing 1,500 copies
ISBN 0 904461 72 6

This edition has been grant aided by North West Arts

Printed by E. Peterson Limited,
12 Laygate, South Shields.

Published and distributed by Ceolfrith Press,
Sunderland Arts Centre, 27 Stockton Road,
Sunderland SR2 7AQ, Tyne & Wear, England.

CONTENTS

- 9 Introduction
- 16 Aw've Hard Wark to Howd up Mi Yed
- 18 To Poverty
- 20 Thee An' Me
- 22 What's to Do 'At Tha'rt Lookin' Soa Sulky, John?
- 24 John Bull An' His Tricks!
- 26 Cheer Up Irish Brothers
- 28 Starved to Death
- 30 What's Up Wi' Thee, Tum?
- 32 Th' Shurat Weaver's Song
- 34 Welcome, Bonny Brid!
- 36 Read At Th' "Bonny Brid's" Wedding Party, 8th November, 1886
- 39 Bowton's Yard
- 41 It's Hard to Ceawer I' Th' Chimney Nook
- 43 Aw've Just Been A-Lookin' At Th' Scholars
- 45 Cheer Up, Toilin' Brothers!
- 47 Mi Gronfeyther
- 49 Mi Gronny
- 51 Mally An' Jonas
- 53 Aw've Turned Mi Bit O'Garden O'er
- 55 Ode to Th' Sun
- 57 Rowl Away, Theaw Grand Owd Ocean
- 60 Bispham
- 62 What! Another Cracked Poet!
- 64 "Only a Poet"
- 66 To A Cricket

Also by Glyn Hughes:

Poetry —

NEIGHBOURS
REST THE POOR STRUGGLER
BEST OF NEIGHBOURS — NEW AND SELECTED POEMS

Prose —

MILLSTONE GRIT
FAIR PROSPECTS

Novel —

WHERE I USED TO PLAY ON THE GREEN (FORTHCOMING, 1982)

LIST OF ILLUSTRATIONS

Front Cover   Samuel Laycock — from *The Collected Writings*, 1900.

Frontispiece   Samuel Laycock aged about 40 years — from *Some Stalybridge Songs and their Singers*, 1944.

p 19   Stalybridge (Cotton Famine) Relief Office.

p 38   'At Number One, Bowton's Yard' from *Warblin's fro' an Owd Songster*, 3rd edn., 1894.

p 50   "We allis meet abeawt one place" from *Warblin's fro' an Owd Songster*, 1893 edn..

p 61   "The Coartin' Neet" from *Warblin's fro' an Owd Songster*, 3rd edn., 1894.

The editor and publisher wish to thank The Tameside Local Studies Library, Stalybridge, for their help in the provision of the illustrations.

SAMUEL LAYCOCK 1826 — 93

Samuel Laycock is one of the best of that gifted school of nineteenth century poets who lived in the cotton towns that lie between Manchester and the Pennines — an area of about thirty miles square where Lancashire, Cheshire, Yorkshire and Derbyshire meet. Oldham, Rochdale, Stalybridge and Failsworth were at its centre. The traditions of their kind of poetry began in the eighteenth century or perhaps earlier, and it is still producing good poems in the work of Harvey Kershaw and others. But its most potent period lasted little longer than a decade, when Laycock wrote almost all of his best work, in between 1856 and 1870 — the period of the American Civil War. The wonder of this poetry, poignant, human, humorous, and produced in a small group of northern industrial towns during a period of harrowing poverty, still goes unappreciated, at any rate by literary people.

Samuel Laycock was born on January 17 1826 (in the same decade as the deaths of Byron, Shelley, Keats and Blake) at a small hill farm at Marsden in the West Riding of Yorkshire. A black millstone-grit place squatting under the wind, amongst sour and sooted grass — but in 1826 the edges of the moors were cultivated and Laycock remembered his home as being more idyllic; he remembered haymaking and a garden

> "Wheer eawr Bobby an' me used to ceawer,
> Eatin' goosbris, and' currans, and ruburb, an' crabs,
> Or owt there were else 'at wur seawer."

Immediately before Sam's birth were the decades of the Yorkshire Luddites, and Marsden was their central district, where with blackened faces they held para-military exercises on the moors at night and raided farmhouses for weapons. On 31 March 1820, two hundred insurgents, unrepentant Luddite survivors from the wholesale executions of 1813, met once again on Hartshead Moor with the intention of "taking" Huddersfield to "establish a free Government". We do not know what Sam Laycock's father, who was a handloom weaver, taught his son about this, or what Samuel felt. The conservatism of the dialect writers has often been noticed. In the words of Martha Vicinns ("The Industrial Muse") "'A hearty good song' replaced insight into the larger problems of life .... The constrictions of an industrial, class-bound society were accepted as part of "life's journey" by dialect writers and their readers". But they were fundamentally insecure poets, with only one foot in the world of the literary-and-philosophical society, whilst the other one remained in the street, or the gutter. In Sam's writing about his childhood, I prefer to see an ironical restraint in these lines written for an audience for whom desperate privation was normal:

SAMUEL LAYCOCK 1826 — 93

> "Aw've often yeard mi fayther tell
> At when aw coom i' th' world misel
> Trade wur slack."

In the world of dialect writing, poet and audience have always understood one another very well. They have been and are close to one another.

At the age of six, Sam spent some time at a day school kept by a Congregational minister, but he was mostly taught to write at Marsden Sunday School. (This was before the churches put a stop to the teaching of writing in Sunday Schools because the lower orders were using their skills to produce radical tracts.) At the age of nine, Laycock was working in a woollen mill from six in the morning until eight at night. Except in the eighteen-sixties, when there was no work for him to do, he worked hard in the mills until his health was ruined. In 1868, at the age of forty-two, his poems had made him a bit of money and he retired to Blackpool, where he was curator of the Whitworth Institute in Fleetwood and developed a reputation as — of all things — a photographer.

In 1837, when Sam was eleven years old, his family left the Pennine moors and came down to the industrial boom-town of Stalybridge in Cheshire. Sam eventually rose to the position of foreman, in mills in Stalybridge and Dukinfield. The 'prefatory sketch' to his collected works, *Warblins Fro' An Owd Songster*, tells us that 'his first effort at rhyming, written on a copticket, was addressed to a fellow operative'. (A copticket is a label attached to a parcel of wool.) He usually wrote his poems quickly and fluently — he wasn't often given the time to write in any other way. He particularly described the composition of one of his finest poems, 'Welcome, Bonny Brid!' as being inspired: he wrote it in one corner of the room where the child, whom he so tenderly but warily welcomed, was being born, and had finished the poem before he discovered that the boy whom he expected was in fact a girl. (However, on the few occasions that we know Laycock laboured over a poem, as with 'Thee and Me', that also seemed to have resulted in his finest work.)

It is said that an evangelical lady asked a child in the 'distressed districts' if she knew 'the meaning of sorrow'. 'Want of cotton' the girl replied. 'Want of cotton' was Laycock's main subject. It was caused by the American Civil War, which closed the Lancashire mills by cutting off supplies of raw material. As a poet, it would have been deeply insulting of Laycock if he had not taken it for granted that his 'public' knew and felt the misery of this as keenly as he himself did, who was also out of work. He considered it his duty, as a poet, to show an honourable way of standing up to the times, rather than to complain about his personal sufferings. He is the opposite of a 'confessional' poet. But it is the pressure of misery that takes Laycock's themes of hearth, home and the domestic joys out of the realm of sentiment and which make his few poems about Nature so tender and even visionary — as in 'Aw've Turned Mi Bit O' Garden O'er'.

SAMUEL LAYCOCK 1826 — 93

Whatever the failings of some of his more famous contemporaries, there is no lack of a realistic understanding of working conditions underlying Laycock's poetry.

Laycock's main weakness springs from the simplicity of his moral and psychological understanding. This lack of breadth hardly damaged his individual best poems, for they are built upon his unique strengths, but we would admire him more and perhaps be able to read through his output at length, if he had tried to get beyond his range. As it was, his vocation collapsed in on itself as soon as he left the industrial town of Stalybridge. Instead of developing his gifts in the leisure of his retirement, this is what happened (The words are those of William E.A. Axon, a writer of 1891):

> " . . . his reputation for facility has brought him into request as a writer of occassional verse for all sorts of celebrations, and he has been expected to plead the cause of bazaars, to welcome the coming, or to speed the parting pastor, to write hymns for the Whit-week celebrations of the Sunday Schools, and addresses for temperance gatherings and Good Templar lodge festivals."

It's not so much that we object to Laycock putting his verses to some use. It's that he came to miss the serious causes of his time and sold out to the secondary ones. Laycock is an example of that process, described by E.P. Thompson in *The Making Of The English Working Class* in which the Nonconformist movements, particularly the Methodists, absorbed and deflated the intellectual life and radical energy of the English working class. Now Laycock's work is in danger of being ignored because of its lack of radical spice. And yet if we do not consider Wordsworth's later apostasy to be detrimental to the body of his earlier work, we must at least extend the same charity to Laycock. But one kind of simplicity leads on to another. Like most dialect poets, or "uneducated" poets (as Southey called them) he stayed too tenaciously in the harbour of the rhyming couplet and other received forms — received from sources that he did not at all properly understand. The metrical forms used by Laycock and other such poets are often as ill-fitting as charity clothing. The poets' contentment, even their pride in them, does not please us — we miss the spirit of resistance and adventure. It took a greater poet, John Clare, to defy the imposition of Latin Grammar upon his inherited English language, to see and resent the exclusiveness of the society which that particular ordering of language represented, and in return to wage a kind of syntactical guerilla-warfare — using 'folk' language-structures to express his alternative understanding of society; using a language free of Latin syntax to express in a nearly-physical way his opposition to enclosures.[1] Let us be charitable to Laycock and remember how remarkable it is that such a man could acquire the skills to write down poetry at all! Awareness of what deftness and sensitivity he did achieve to handle the range of styles exemplified in this selection, might make it seem a miracle.

That is if we did not take into account the strong culture of oral poetry that was bursting with life in Stalybridge and the other cotton towns at this period. (And it is still kept alive, by people who can recite dialect verse by the hour; and by, for instance, the Oldham Tinkers, who add new poems to the tradition and **perform** the older ones, the work of Laycock, Waugh and Fitton, better perhaps than they have ever been performed.) Laycock learnt the art of poetry through such poems as 'Th' Owdham Weaver', 'Th' Man at Mester Grundy's', 'John O'Grinfield' and 'Droylsden Wakes Song'. All these ballads dealt with what the dialect-poets called 'homely subjects' — industrial life from the operative's point of view; the comfort and love to be found, or at least hoped for, on the poor man's hearth whilst the dogs of hunger and poverty prowl outside; and pathetic dreams of escape, usually by enlisting to fight "oather French, Dutch, or Spanish, to me it's o' one. (More savagely radical ballads are rare. They were probably too compromising for their possessors to keep them.)

Laycock basically thought of himself as an oral poet, he called himself a 'songster' and his poems 'lyrics'. The working people of Lancashire thought so too; there was such a huge audience for sheet ballads that could be sung or recited, that in 1864 at the time of the 'cotton panic' no less than 14,000 people who were near starvation thought it worth a penny or twopence to buy Laycock's poems. (To put that into perspective: about this time, a committee of mill masters in Huddersfield found that approximately half the population of the town was living off an average of twopence per day per person.)

Nonetheless, Laycock's poems **were** written down. Brian Hollingworth (in *Songs of the People*, Manchester University Press 1977) argues that the great decade of dialect writing occurred at the point when it passed from an oral to a written tradition, and before education acts and general literacy made dialect writing 'an antiquarian and rather nostalgic attempt to conserve a dying culture'. The opportunity for education was embraced as an opportunity to be **free** of local, dialect culture, and the dialect poets then became entrenched in the defensive, nostalgic positions in which they are still to be found. The flowering was so brief and the decay had been so long; and it is from the later nostalgic part of the tradition that widespread prejudices against the dialect poets have arisen. It is perhaps Lancashire's other famous tradition — that of comedians and self-mockers — that is the cause of us immediately laughing and giving up at sight of those clotted phonetic renderings, with which the ill-educated struggled to make an oral tradition available and respected by 'English Letters'. Meanwhile the borrowed language, the borrowed poetic stanzas, from Burns in particular, played havoc with the poets' true intentions.

But the very best dialect poets do rise above this sometimes, and I have made my selection of Laycock partly to show his range and his sensitivity to various poetic opportunities. Only a master poet could have handled the steady, sorrowful, patient tread of the verse that is so suitable for 'Aw've Hard Wark To Howd Up Mi Yed', and not once let it slip into leaden prose. It takes a fine poet to personify 'Poverty' as well as Laycock has done it; to write so naturally and fluently about the happenings of an ordinary day, as in 'Aw've Turned Mi Bit O' Garden O'er'; to make such original verse out of the neo-Elizabethianism of 'Bispham' (one of Laycock's good later poems, and written in Blackpool — and which I have included for this reason, although its sentiments are, at bottom, trite) Sometimes Laycock's background almost automatically fed originality into his verse, as when he wittily and half-humorously compares the noise of the ocean to, of all things, the row of a non-conformist meeting ('Rowl Away, Theaw Grand Owd Ocean'). Within his range also is what today we would call 'committed verse': admittedly not such good poetry as that he wrote from his personal experience of the 1860s, but saved by a fine use of irony in '"What's To Do 'At Tha'rt Lookin' Soa Sulky, John?"'; a witness to Laycock's far-sighted hatred of John Bull's imperialism and hypocritical Evangelism, and witness also to Laycock's wider sympathies beyond Lancashire, with the Irish and the other British colonials.

To put Laycock in a literary perspective, his most consistently high quality poetry, his *Lancashire Lyrics (Twelve In Number) Written During The Cotton Panic* was composed in Stalybridge in the eighteen-sixties, just after the deaths of Wordsworth and Coleridge. His living rivals were Bryant, Landor, Clare, Tennyson, Browning, Emily Brontë, Arnold, D.G. and Christina Rossetti, Morris, Swinburne, Thomson, Lanier, Patmore, Meredith, Hopkins, Bridges and Hardy. I take these names from a well-known Penguin anthology — in which, of course, Laycock is not included. Yet, in my opinion, not at all of these eighteen poets can be considered definitely as Laycock's superiors. He is at least the equal of many in craftsmanship, originality, range, and in the power of his verse to move his readers' emotions. And who betters him in terms of writing about the actual life that was lived by most Englishmen at that time? If I can at least rescue what might be called his masterpiece, 'Welcome Bonny Brid!' out of limbo so that it might — who knows — begin to appear in general anthologies of English poetry, this selection of Laycock's verse will be well-justified.

Laycock was well enough appreciated by the audience that he first of all had in mind — not only the 14,000 people who bought his broadsheets, but also those who purchased three thousand copies of his collected poems, *Warblin's Fro' An Owd Songster* in 1893 and 1894 — a handsome and substantial book, published and sold in Oldham where now it is probably difficult to sell even a single copy of any decent verse collection.

But from the very beginning, those who dominated the national culture ignored Laycock's poetry; or if they praised it, they did so in such an insulting way that it might, you would think, break the heart of a sensitive man. 'We like to see men of his class engaged in any kind of intellectual labour advantageous to themselves, and stimulating to their fellows'. (It kept them occupied and out of mischief, no doubt.) In 1864 the 'Weekly Review' said: 'Any work which tends, in however slight a degree, to the moral and intellectual improvement of the labouring and artizan class is deserving of every consideration.'

Laycock was insulted in the same way as was John Clare. If we fail to appreciate such poets as Hopkins and Hardy, Clare and William Barnes — all poets who, for different reasons, gave up the expectation of being heard in the dominant culture — the loss is mostly ours. Here is my attempt to present a fine, neglected poet.

Glyn Hughes

[1] For a fuller account of this, see John Barrell *The Idea of Landscape and the Sense of Place 1730 — 1840,* Cambridge Univ. Press 1972.

AW'VE HARD WARK TO HOWD UP MI YED

WHEEREVER aw trudge neaw-a-days,
    Aw'm certain to see some owd friend
Lookin' anxiously up i' my face,
    An' axin' when times are beawn t' mend.
Aw'm surprised heaw folk live, aw declare,
    Wi' th' clammin' an' starvin' they'n stood;
God bless 'em, heaw patient they are!
    Aw wish aw could help 'em, aw would.

But really aw've nowt aw con give,
    Except it's a bit ov a song,
An' th' Muses han hard wark to live,
    One's bin hamper'd an' powfagg'd so long;
Aw've tried to look cheerful an' bowd,
    An' yo know what aw've written an' said,
But iv truth mun be honestly towd,
    Aw've hard wark to howd up mi yed!

There'll be some on us missin' aw deawt
    Iv there isn't some help for us soon;
We'n bin jostled an' tumbled abeawt,
    Till we're welly o knocked eawt o' tune;
Eawr Margit, hoo frets an' hoo cries,
    As hoo sits theer, wi' th' choilt on her knee
An' aw connot blame th' lass, for hoo tries
    To be cheerful an' gradely wi' me.

Yon Yankees may think it's rare fun,
    Kickin' up sich a shindy o'th' globe;
Confound 'em, aw wish they'd get done,
    For they'd weary eawt th' patience o' Job!
We shall have to go help 'em, that's clear,
    Iv they dunno get done very soon;
Iv eawr Volunteers wur o'er theer,
    They'd sharpen 'em up to some tune.

Neaw it's hard for a mortal to tell
   Heaw long they may plague us this road;
Iv they'd hurt nob'dy else but thersel,
   They met fo eawt and feight till they'rn stow'd.
Aw think it's high time someb'dy spoke,
   When so many are cryin' for bread;
For there's hundreds an' theawsands o' folk,
   Deawn i' Lancashire hardly hawve fed.

Th' big men, when they yer eawr complaint,
   May treat it as "gammon" an' "stuff",
An' tell us we use to' much paint,
   But we dunnot daub paint on enuff,
If they think it's noan true what we sen,
   Ere they charge us wi' tellin' a lie,
Let 'em look into th' question loike men,
   An' come deawn here a fortnit an' try.

TO POVERTY

TH'RT here again, well, come this way;
We'n bin owd chums for mony a day;
We'n often differed when we'n met,
But never had a partin' yet.
Aw conno say awm fond o' thee,
Then why does t' stick so fast to me?
Aw know aw used t' be some an' mad,
Theau plagued me so when aw're a lad.

Tha knows that time when Robin Clegg
Fell off th' barn dur an' broke his leg?
Poor lad! aw took him on mi knee,
An' should ha' helped him but for thee.
What con a body do 'at's poor?
Aw cried a bit, but nowt no moor.
Well, never moind, he geet it set,
An' thee an' me are owd chums yet.

Aw've tried for years to shake thee off —
An' when th' last winter theaw'd a cough,
Aw hoped to see thee laid i' th' greawnd,
But th' summer weather's browt thee reawnd.
Well, poo thi cheer up — warm thi shanks,
Aw'll sit an' watch thee play thi pranks;
Aw meon to shunt thee when aw con,
Till then aw'll face thee like a mon.

Thae'll ha' fair play, tha needn't fear —
Now, now, thae'll see no shufflin' here!
Aw'll tell thee plainly theaw'rt a pest,
An's spoilt me mony a good neet's rest;
Theaw stole mi supper t'other neet,
An' sent me t' bed wi' cowd wet feet.
Aw didn't relish this — Would theaw?
Well, come, we'll let it pass o'er neaw.

Heaw is it theaw ne'er goes to see
Big folks 'at's better off nor me?
There's plenty up an' deawn i'th' lond,
'At theaw'd do weel to tak' bi' th' hond,
An' leod 'em every day to schoo'.
There's young Nat Wild — poor silly foo' —
He's lots o' brass, but noan mich wit,
Go play thi pranks wi' him a bit.

Aw've had mi friends — fond, firm, an' true,
An' dear relations not a few;
But noan o' these han stuck to me
As firmly an' as long as thee.
An' after o it's hardly reet
To goa an' turn thee eawt i' th' street,
And one not knowin' wheer tha'rt beawn
Aw conno do it — sit thee deawn.

THEE AN' ME

THA'RT livin' at thi country seat,
   Among o th' gents an' nobs;
Tha's sarvant girls to cook thi meat,
   An' do thi bits o' jobs.
Aw'm lodgin' here wi' Bridget Yates,
   At th' cot near th' Ceaw Lone Well;
Aw mend mi stockins, peel th' potatoes,
   An' wesh mi shurts misel'!

Tha wears a finer cooat nor me;
   Thi purse is better lined,
An' fortin's lavished moor o' thee,
   Than th' rest o' human kind.
Life's storms 'at rage abeawt this yead,
   An' pelt so hard at me —
That mony a time aw've wished aw're dead, —
   But seldom trouble thee.

Tha'rt rich i' ole this world can give;
   Tha's silver, an' tha's gowd;
But me — aw find it hard to live,
   Aw'm poor, an' gettin' owd.
These fields an' lones aw'm ramblin' throo —
   They o belong to thee;
Aw've only just a yard or two
   To ceawer in when aw dee.

When tha rides eawt th' folks o areawnd
   Stond gapin' up at thee,
Becose tha'rt worth ten theawsand peawnd',
   But scarcely notice me.
Aw trudge abeawt fro' spot to spot,
   An' nob'dy seems to care:
They never seek my humble cot,
   To ax me heaw aw fare.

If tha should dee, there's lots o' folk
   Would fret an' cry, noa deawt;
When aw shut up, they'll only joke,
   An' say, "He's just gone eawt!

Well, never heed him, let him goo,
   An' find another port;
We're never to a chap or two,
   We've plenty moor o' th' sort."

Tha'll have a stone placed o'er thi grave
   To show thi name an' age;
An o tha's done 'at's good an' brave,
   Be seen o' history's page.
When aw get tumbled into th' greawnd,
   There'll ne'er be nowt to show
Who's restin' 'neath that grassy meawnd,
   An' nob'dy'll want to know.

But deawn i' th' grave, what spoils o th' sport,
   No ray o' leet can shine;
An' th' worms 'll have hard wark to sort
   Thy pampered clay fro' mine.
So, when this world for th' next tha swaps,
   Tak' wi' thee under th' stone
Thi cooat ov arms, an' bits o' traps,
   Or else tha'll ne'er be known.

Pack up thi albert, hoop, an' pin,
   An' opera-glass an' o;
Be sure tha sees 'em o put in,
   Before tha gangs below.
Then iv some hungry worm should come,
   To root abeawt thi bones, —
Tha may stond a better chance nor some
   If it's known tha'rt Mister Jones.

But up above there's One at sees
   Thro' th' heart o' every mon;
An' He'll just find thee as tha dees,
   So dee as well as t'con.
An' when deawn here this campin' ends,
   An' o eawr fau'ts forgiven, —
Let thee an' me still shew we're friends,
   Bi shakin' honds i' Heaven!

WHAT'S TO DO 'AT THA'RT LOOKIN' SOA SULKY, JOHN?

WHAT'S to do at tha'rt lookin' soa sulky?
   Are th' Radicals provin' unkoind?
Tha seems very much eawt o' flunter,
   As iv tha'd some weight on thi moind.
Tha wanted these Tories to govern;
   They're governin' neaw doesta see;
Soa dunno thee run thi own wark deawn,
   Tha's sent 'em, so let 'em a-be.

The've mended thy sink-holes wi' "Science,"
   An' they want to mend other foalks' to';
They've th' Suez Canal to slutch yet, mon,
   An' then they've got Cyprus to do.
Look what millions o' foalk are i' darkness —
   Beawt Bible, beawt devil, beawt leet;
An' are we to leov 'em i' this way?
   Nay, nay, John, that wouldn't be reet.

It's wrong to be graspin' an' selfish,
   Soa John, lad, let's try to do fair;
Iv its only a devil we're blest wi',
   Let's goa an' tak' th' heathens a share.
They send us their rice an' their cotton,
   To keep these frail bodies i' tune;
Let's give them some peawder an' bullets,
   To prepare 'em for th' mansions aboon!

What ailsto? tha seems very restless!
   Oh, aw see, it's thi conscience at works;
Tha'rt thinkin' abeawt thoose Bulgarians,
   'At wur slaughtered bi th' Russians an' th' Turks.
Neaw, why should theaw bother o'er these things? —
   Look here — keep thi heart up, owd brid;
Tha never encouraged these butchers
   To goa an' to do as they did.

Thee be easy; tha'll live a deol longer;
    Dunno fret abeawt th' wrongs 'at tha sees:
For tha connot get roses fro' thistles
    Iv tha bothers thisel' till tha dees.
There's evil i' th' world, an' there will be;
    An' it's folly thee crackin' thi brains;
For ole tha con do will be useless,
    An' tha'll only get kicked for thi pains.

What's th' use o' foalks botherin' their noddles
    Or bein' at th' trouble to think,
So long as there's plenty to stur on,
    I' th' shape o' meyt, bacco, an' drink.
Look heaw grogsellers fatten an' flourish;
    Look heaw th' brewers are macking their "tin";
Neaw they never get favoured i' this way,
    When th' Radical government's in.

Look what toimes workin'-men con have neaw, mon;
    What lockeawts, an' turneawts, an' stroikes!
Iv tha's sense tha'll keep things as they are, John,
    For a chap can do just as he loikes.
Thee keep goin' on as theaw has done;
    Never argue thi principles eawt;
But up wi' thi first when tha'rt tackled.
    An' fot thi opponents a cleawt.

It's noa business o' thoine to be thinkin';
    Leov that job to thoose 'at have brains;
Thee get on wi' thi workin' an' drinkin',
    Worship th' tyrant at' forges thi chains.
Shoot thi nayburs, to mak 'em respect thee;
    Never mind abeawt doin' what's reet;
Tha connot booath serve God an' Mammon,
    So tha's no need to try, mon. — Good neet.

JOHN BULL AN' HIS TRICKS!

OH, forshame on thee, John! forshame on thee, John!
   The murderin' owd thief at theaw art:
Tha'rt a burnin' disgrace to humanity, mon,
   Tho' theaw thinks thisel' clever an' smart.
Tha'rt a beggar for sendin' eawt Bibles an' beer,
   An' calling it "Civilization";
While thee an' thi dear Christian countrymen here,
   Are chettin' an' lyin' like station.

Thee tak' my advoice, John, an' get a good brush,
   An' sweep well abeawt thi own door;
An' put th' bit o' th' lond at tha's stown to some use,
   Ere theaw offers to steal ony moor.
An' let th' heathens a-be; for tha's no need to fear
   'At they're loikely to get into hell:
My opinion is this — if there's onyone near
   A place o' that mack — it's thisel'.

It's thee 'at aw meon, John, theaw hypocrite, theaw;
   Wi' thi Sundayfied, sanctified looks!
Doesta think 'at ole th' milk comes fro' th' paps o' thy ceaw!
   Is ole th' wisdom beawnd up i' thy books!
An' what abeawt th' mixture o' cotton an' clay,
   'At theaw thrusts on thi unwillin' nayburs?
Eh John, tha'rt a "Cure", but tha'll catch it some day,
   When tha's ended these damnable labours.

Tha may weel tell the Lord what a wretch theaw art, John,
   For tha pulls a long face on a Sunday;
An', to prove what tha says, tha does o' 'at tha con
   To rob thi poor nayburs on th' Monday.
What business has theaw to go battin' thi wings,
   An' crowin' on other folks' middin?
Doesta think thi black brothers sich mean cringin' things
   As to give up their whoams at thy biddin'?

An' tha's th' cheek to thank God, when tha meets wi' success,
    As iv He stooped to sanction sich wark!
Neaw one would ha' thowt 'at tha couldn't ha' done less
    Than to keep sich loike actions i' th' dark.
Iv tha meons to go on wi' committin' these sins —
    Sins tha'll ne'er get weshed eawt or forgiven —
Tha should try to keep matters as quiet as tha con,
    An' ne'er let em' know up i' Heaven.

Tha wur allus a bullyead, i' thi best o' thi days,
    An' this ole thi nayburs must know;
An', tho' tha seems pious, an' pulls a long face,
    They con manage to see through it o.
But when tha goes sneakin' an' tries to cheat God,
    It strikes me tha'rt goin' to' far.
Aw'm noan mitch surproised at thi impudence, John;
    Aw'm only surprised heaw tha dar!

What business has theaw to be sendin' eawt thieves,
    To steal slices off other foalks' bread?
It would look better on thee to rowl up thi sleeves,
    An' work for thi livin' instead.
Aw' tell thi what John — an' tak' notice o' this —
    Tha ne'er knew a nation to thrive,
Wheer th' bees preferred feightin' to good honest wark; —
    They're like drones stealin' honey fro' th' hive!

Iv tha's th' sense ov a jackass tha'll tarry awhoam,
    An' keep th' own garden i' fettle;
But tha'd rather be eawt wi' thi Bible an' gun,
    An' robbin' some other mon's kettle.
Neaw drop these mean tricks — this contemptible wrong,
    An' behave a bit more loike a mon;
Or aw'll gie thee another warm dose before long,
    For aw'm gradely ashamed on thee, John!

CHEER UP IRISH BROTHERS

CHEER up a bit, poor Irish brethren,
  Tho' it's hard wark to do so awm sure;
One's surprised yo'n kept up as yo' have done,
  Wi' th' hardships yo'n had to endure.
What wi' soldiers, police, an' coercion,
  Imprisonment, buckshot, an' fines;
An' land agents sneakin' areawnd yo',
  Yo'n certainly very hard lines.

Well, try to hold on a bit longer;
  Stand firm, neaw 'at help seems so near;
We're feightin' yo'r battles i' England,
  An' shall win 'em, yo'n no need to fear.
Let me tele yo' we're gettin' on grandly;
  We've some rare intellectual fights;
Morley, Sir William Harcourt, an' others,
  Are battlin' reet hard for yo'r rights.

We're aware what yo'r patriots are sufferin' —
  What vengeance is piled on their yeads;
Heaw they're treated as murderers an' felons,
  Thrown i' prison, wi' planks for their beds.
But, tak' heart, mi poor sufferin' brothers,
  There's room e'en for th' Tories to mend;
When they'll stoop to go steal a chap's breeches
  They must be abeawt at th' far end.

It's a queer game for statesmen to play at —
  A mean sort o' business, for sure;
But it needn't cause very mitch wonder,
  We've been guilty o' stealin' befoor.
Eawr Tory friends call it "annexin'" —
  A rayther fine sort ov a name;
An' yet, when one looks at th' job fairly,
  It's thievin', pure thievin', ole th' same.

We're noted througheawt ole creation
  For convertin' black niggers an' Jews;
We mak' 'em respect us, aw'll tell yo';
  Or "pepper" those weel 'at refuse.
We've been tryin' that game on i' Ireland —
  For eighty long years, an' moor;
But, someheaw, this treatment doesn't suit yo —
  It's a med'cine 'at doesn't seem t' cure.

God help yo'! an' may yo' have patience;
  For it's certainly very "hard cheese"
To be treated as yo'r bein' treated,
  Wi' vain, heartless men like these.
Well, tho' they're so clever at braggin',
  Yo'll think they're abeawt at th' last shift,
Neaw they've stolen yo'r pigs an' potatoes,
  Burnt yo'r hovels, an' turned yo' adrift.

Yo'n long been i' th' wilderness, weepin',
  An' mournful an' sad's been yo'r song;
But leet's breakin' forth at th' horizon,
  An' th' sun will be up before long.
Get yo'r harps, 'at have long lain i' silence,
  An' prepare for a merrier tune;
For th' daisies will oppen i' th' spring time,
  An' there's sure to be roses i' June.

STARVED TO DEATH

STARVED to death, did you say? dear a-me!
Why, bless us, wheerever i'th' world could it be?
Wur he somewheer i' Greenland, wheer th' north
winds blow?
Or ramblin' o'er th' moors, an' lost i'th' snow?
Or wur he away i' some lonely place,
Wheer th' sun seldom shoines on a human face;
I' some far-away desert 'at's seldom trod —
Wheer th' soil appears fresh fro' th' hands o' God?

Nay, nay he're noan starved on a foreign strand,
But here, awhom, i' this Christian land,
Wheer th' seawnd o'th' church-goin' bell is heard,
An' charity's preached in the name of eawr Lord.
Wheer the priest an' the Levite on luxuries dine.
An' nowbles an' statesmen get fuddled wi' wine;
It wur here, i' owd England, this "Queen of the Isles" —
This garden o' eawrs, on which Providence smiles.

It wur here 'at he deed, — i'th' lond ov his birth; —
I'th' wealthiest city on God's fair earth.
Starved to death within seet an' seawnd
O'th' merchant princes 'at prosper areawnd!
Ah, starved to death in a Christian land.
Eh dear! this is hard to understand —
Yore brother an mine lyin' stiff an' cowd,
In a city o' splendour, a mart o' gowd.

Starved to death! a loife flung away!
God's image starved eawt o'th' poor vessel o' clay:
A dear choilt o' somb'dy's, a brother o' eawers,
Wi' similar feelin's an' mental peawers,
Thrown away as iv nothin' worth;
Not one friend to assist him on ole God's earth.
O, brothers an' sisters, pray what can we do?
O, thinkers an' writers — here's sum'at for you.

Come, thunner it eawt i' clarion tones,
'At we're starvin' th' bees while we pamper th' drones.
Thunner it eawt, an' let it be known,
Fro' th' pauper i'th' warkheawse to th' queen on th' throne.
We can boast o' eawr greatness an' prowess i' war,
An' eawr fame as a nation's oft' talked of afar;
An' shall it, wi' truth, o' owd England be said,
That her sons an' her dowters are starvin' for bread?

Is this what we co feedin' th' hungry an' th' dry,
Or doin' to others as we'd be done by?
Nay, we rayther think not; we should think it wur queer
If we'rn deein o' hunger, an' nob'dy came near.
While one's livin' i' "clover", he's friends ole reawned;
Iv he's crush'd wi' misfortune, they're hard to be feawnd.
Let us rectify ole these sad blunders, an' try
To be brothers i' sorrow as weel as i' joy.

Yo' 'at preitch Christ's religion, come, practise it too;
Here's a field for yore labour, — here's sum'at to do:
Look abeawt on th' wayside for some witherin' fleawer,
An' give it o' th' help 'at may lie i' yore peawer.
Dunno fall into th' error o' wastin' yore breath,
I' talkin' to th' hungry o' judgment an' death;
If yore fishin' for souls, yo'n a very poor bait;
Yo'll be loiklier to catch 'em wi' sum'at to ate.

We met as weel talk to a chap 'at's noan reet,
An' tell folk to walk 'at's lost th' use o' their feet,
As attempt to feed th' hungry wi' orthodox creeds,
Or quieten a stomach wi' crosses an' beads.
Let's scorn to insult wi' sich simperin' cant,
As to talk abeawt deein' to folk 'at's i' want;
Let us act moor loike Christians, an' every one strive
To let 'em have sum'at to keep 'em alive.

WHAT'S UP WI' THEE, TUM?

MON, tha howds deawn thi yead loike a thief,
   An tha's noan getten th' pluck ov a leawse;
Neaw, what's th' use on thee nursin' thi grief?
   Ger up, or aw'll give thee a seawse:
Mon, tha'rt welly a shawm to be seen,
   Are ta meawtin', or what does ta ail?
Come, mop up that weet fro' thi een,
   For aw've browt thee some bacon and male.

"Aw dar say tha'rt hungry, owd lad,
   An thi woife, theer, hoo looks like a ghost;
Yo'r Jonathan's welly as bad,
   An yo're Nelly, poor thing, hoo looks lost.
Hast a bit ov a pon ony wheer,
   'At 'll fry yo' a collop or two?
An aw'll run for a pint o' smo' beer,
   Fro' owd Mally Dawson's i' th' broo."

"Ne'er mind, Jim, we need no smo' drink;
   We can manage beawt swillin' it deawn;
An, thank thee, aw mony a toime think
   Tha'rt th' best-natured chap i' this teawn.
God bless thee, an' thank thee ogen;
   Iv it wur not for thee an' yo're Sam
Bringin' summat to eat, neaw an then,
   Aw believe we should o have to clam.

"This mornin' owd Alice, th' next dur,
   Coom in wi' a potful o' tay;
An' oh, some an' thankful we wur,
   For it's o we'n had t' live on to-day.
Aw've bin eawt a beggin' sin noon,
   Just look heaw mi stockins are wet;
It's wi' havin' big holes i' mi shoon,
   But tha knows, Jim, they're th' best one can get."

"Well, well, lad, aw know heaw yo' are,
    An aw'm noan so mich better mysel';
Heaw long aw may have eawt to spare
    It's hard for a body to tell;
But as long as aw've getten owt t' give
    Tha'rt sure to be one aw shall sarve;
Aw shall help an owd shopmate to live,
    An' see 'at tha'rt noan left to starve.

"Send yo're Nelly to th' cobblers to neet—
    Aw meon cobbler Jack's deawn i'th' fowd —
An' aw'll beigh thi some shoon to thi feet,
    For tha'rt gettin' thi deoth wi cowd;
An' aw'll speak to owd Mistress Scholes,
    To look th' woife up a bit ov a dress;
For that hoo has on's full o' holes —
    But hoo's getten nowt better, aw guess.

"Neaw, Tum, lad, tha'rt cryin' aw see,
    Come, cheer up as weel as tha con;
Tha's noan bin forgotten, tha'll see;
    There's foalk as con feel for thee, mon.
Tha's noan bin beawt trouble, aw know;
    It's no wonder to me tha should fret;
But there's room i'th' world yet for us o
    Mon; tha's no need to hang thisel yet.

"Tum! aw knew thee when tha wur a lad,
    Livin' th' next dur but one to th' Breawn Ceaw;
Thi heart then wur leetsome an' glad;
    What aw want is — to see it so neaw.
Tha'rt welcome to my little mite,
    For aw connot afford a big sum;
But as long as aw've getten a bite,
    Tha shall ha' th' hawve on't — that tha shall, Tum."

TH' SHURAT WEAVER'S SONG

CONFOUND it! aw ne'er wur so woven afore,
Mi back's welly brocken, mi fingers are sore;
Aw've bin starin' an' rootin' among this Shurat,
Till aw'm very near getten as bloint as a bat.

Every toime aw go in wi' mi cuts to owd Joe,
He gies mi a cursin', an' bates mi an' o;
Aw've a warp i' one loom wi' booath selvedges marr'd,
An' th' other's as bad for he's dress'd it to' hard.

Aw wish aw wur fur enuff off, eawt o' th' road,
For o' weavin' this rubbitch aw'm gettin' reet stow'd;
Aw've nowt i' this world to lie deawn on but straw,
For aw've only eight shillin' this fortni't to draw.

Neaw aw haven't mi family under mi hat,
Aw've a woife an' six childer to keep eawt o' that;
So aw'm rayther among it at present yo see,
Iv ever a fellow wur puzzled, it's me!

Iv one turns eawt to steal, folk 'll co me a thief,
An' aw conno' put th' cheek on to ax for relief;
As aw said i' eawr heawse, t' other neet to mi woife,
Aw never did nowt o' this sort i' mi loife.

One doesn't like everyone t' know heaw they are,
But we'n suffered so long thro' this 'Merica war,
'At there's lot's o' poor factory folk getten t' fur end,
An' they'll soon be knock'd o'er iv th' toimes don't mend.

Oh, dear! iv yon Yankees could only just see
Heaw they're clemmin' an' starvin' poor weavers loike me,
Aw think they'd soon settle their bother, an' strive
To send us some cotton to keep us alive.

There's theawsands o' folk just i' th' best o' their days,
Wi' traces o' want plainly seen i' their face;
An' a future afore 'em as dreary an' dark,
For when th' cotton gets done we shall o be beawt wark.

We'n bin patient an' quiet as long as we con;
Th' bits o' things we had by us are welly o gone;
Aw've bin trampin' so long, mi owd shoon are worn eawt,
An' mi halliday clooas are o on 'em "up th' speawt".

It wur nobbut last Monday aw sowd a good bed —
Nay, very near gan it — to get us some bread;
Afore these bad times cum aw used to be fat,
But neaw, bless yo'r loife, aw'm as thin as a lat!

Mony a toime i' mi loife aw've seen things lookin' feaw,
But never as awk'ard as what they are neaw;
Iv there isn't some help for us factory folk soon,
Aw'm sure we shall o be knocked reet eawt o' tune.

Come give us a lift, yo' 'at han owt to give,
An' help yo're poor brothers an' sisters to live;
Be kind, an' be tender to th' needy an' poor,
An' we'll promise when th' times mend we'll ax yo' no moor.

WELCOME, BONNY BRID!

TH'ART welcome, little bonny brid,
But shouldn't ha' come just when tha did;
    Toimes are bad.
We're short o' pobbies for eawr Joe,
But that, of course, tha didn't know,
    Did ta, lad?

Aw've often yeard mi feyther tell,
'At when aw coom i' th' world misel'
    Trade wur slack;
An' neaw it's hard wark pooin' throo —
But aw munno fear thee, iv aw do
    Tha'll go back.

Cheer up! these toimes'll awter soon;
Aw'm beawn to beigh another spoon —
    One for thee;
An', as tha's sich a pratty face
Aw'll let thee have eawr Charley's place
    On mi knee.

God bless thee, love, aw'm fain tha'rt come,
Just try an' mak' thisel awhoam:
    Here's thi nest;
Tha'rt loike thi mother to a tee,
But tha's thi feyther's nose, aw see,
    Well, aw'm blest!

Come, come tha needn't look so shy,
Aw am no' blamin' thee, not I;
    Settle deawn,
An' tak' this haupney for thisel,
There's lots o' sugar-sticks to sell
    Deawn i' th' teawn.

Aw know when furst aw coom to th' leet,
Aw're fond o' owt' at tasted sweet;
    Tha'll be th' same.
But come, tha's never towd thi dad
What he's to co thee yet, mi lad —
    What's thi name?

Hush! hush! tha mustn't cry this way,
But get this sope o' cinder tay
    While it's warm;
Mi mother used to give it me,
When aw wur sich a lad as thee,
    In her arm.

Hush-a-babby, hush-a-bee, —
Oh, what a temper! dear-a-me
    Heaw tha skrikes!
Here's a bit o' sugar, sithee;
Howd thi noise, an' then aw'll gie thee
    Owt tha likes.

We've nobbut getten coarsish fare,
But, eawt o' this tha'll get thi share,
    Never fear.
Aw hope tha'll never want a meal,
But allis fill thi bally weel
    While tha'rt here.

Thi feyther's noan been wed so long,
An' yet tha sees he's middlin' throng
    Wi' yo' o.
Besides thi little brother Ted,
We've one upsteers, asleep i' bed,
    Wi' eawr Joe.

But tho' we've childer two or three,
We'll mak' a bit o' reawm for thee,
    Bless thee, lad!
Tha'rt th' prattiest brid we have i' th' nest,
So hutch up closer to mi breast;
    Aw'm thi dad.

READ AT
TH' "BONNY BRID'S" WEDDING PARTY,
8th NOVEMBER, 1886

WELL, Schofield, tha'rt welcome to Hannah;
    Tho' awm troubled a bit, as tha'll see;
But if there's one moor nor another
    'At th' lass will be safe wi', it's thee.
For twenty-three years, or near on it,
    Aw've had th' pleasure o' callin her mine;
But tha's 'ticed her away fro' my brid-cage,
    An' coaxed her to go into thine.

Well, bless her! aw've done th' best aw could do,
    An' noa deawt tha intends to do th' same.
Let's hope 'at hoo's made a good bargain
    I' changin' her cage an' her name.
When hoo gets to her whoam at New Moston,
    May her nayburs eawt theer be as kind
An' as anxious to mak' her feel happy,
    As thoose 'at hoo's leavin' behind.

Neaw, it's pleasant to ha' one's good wishes,
    An' these yo'll tak' with yo', awm sure;
An' what is there moor to feel preawd on,
    Than a hearty "God bless yo'!" fro th' poor.
A lovin' an' good mother's blessin'
    Is o' far greater value nor gowd;
Yo may find human natur i' th' crescent,
    But yo'll find a deol moor on't i' th' fowd!

Two year' sin' tha sought my acquaintance,
    An' admired oather me or mi song;
At least tha pretended to do so;
    But aw saw throo thi game ole along.
We had eawr nice walks in a mornin',
    An' mi company then wur o reet;
But there's one little matter aw noticed,
    Thi een wur on th' brid-cage at neet!

It's o very weel to be laffin',
   But youth allis did laff at age;
Tha'rt desarvin' a reet deawn good thrashin'
   For stealin' my brid eawt o' th' cage.
Well, ne'er mind; iv tha'rt suited tha'rt welcome;
   Aw've noa deawt but thi motives are pure;
So aw'll not ha' thee ta'en up for robb'ry
   If tha'll promise to do it no moor.

These presents fro' friends an' fro' nayburs
   Are expressive o' love an' good-will;
They're ole very pratty an' useful,
   An' some on 'em samples o' skill.
When they get to "Rose Cottage", New Moston,
   They cannot but serve to remind
O' th years 'at yo' spent here at Blackpool,
   Wi' thoose 'at your leavin' behind.

We shall think an yo' kindly an' often,
   Altho' yo're away eawt o' th' seet:
We shall miss Hannah's footsteps on th' threshold;
   We shall miss, too, her well-known "good neet".
Well, yo' go wi' a father's good wishes;
   Yo're united for better or worse;
Yo'll booath ha' to draw i' one harness,
   An' join at one bed, an' one purse.

An' neaw — just one word to those present —
   Aw'm fairly surprised, aw must own,
At th' manner yo'n treated th' young couple,
   An' th' good naybourly feelin' yo'n shown.
Yon flung a few fleawers i' life's pathway,
   An' Royalty couldn't do moor;
These presents, kind words, an' good wishes,
   Will long be remembered, aw'm sure.

38

BOWTON'S YARD

AT number one, i' Bowton's yard, mi gronny keeps a skoo,
But hasn't mony scholars yet, hoo's only one or two;
They sen th' owd woman's rather cross, — well, well,
    it may be so;
Aw know hoo box'd me rarely once, an' pood mi ears an' o.

At number two lives widow Burns — hoo weshes clooas for folk;
Their Billy, that's her son, gets jobs at wheelin' coke;
They sen hoo coarts wi' Sam-o'-Neds, 'at lives at number three;
It may be so, aw conno tell, it matters nowt to me.

At number three, reet facin' th' pump, Ned Grimshaw keeps a
    shop;
He's Eccles-cakes, an' gingerbread, an' treacle beer, an' pop;
He sells oat-cakes an' o, does Ned, he has boath soft an' hard,
An' everybody buys off him 'at lives i' Bowton's yard.

At number four Jack Blunderick lives; he goes to th' mill an'
    wayves;
An' then, at th' week-end, when he's time, he pows a bit an'
    shaves;
He's badly off, is Jack, poor lad; he's rayther lawm, they sen,
An' his childer keep him deawn a bit — aw think they'n nine or ten.

At number five aw live mysel', wi' owd Susanah Grimes,
But dunno loike so very weel — hoo turns me eawt sometimes;
An' when awm in there's ne'er no leet, aw have to ceawer i' th'
    dark;
Aw conno pay mi lodgin' brass, becose awm eawt o' wark.

At number six, next dur to us, an' close o' th' side o' th' speawt,
Owd Susie Colins sells smo' drink, but hoo's welly allis beawt;
But heaw it is that is the case aw'm sure aw conno' tell,
Hoo happen maks it very sweet, an' sups it o hersel'!

At number seven there's nob'dy lives, they left it yesterday,
Th' bum-baylis coom an' mark'd their things, and took 'em o away;
They took 'em in a donkey-cart — aw know nowt wheer they went —
Aw recon they'n bin ta'en and sowd becose they owed some rent.

At number eight — they're Yawshur folk — there's only th' mon an' woife,
Aw think aw ne'er seed nicer folk nor these i' o mi loife;
Yo'll never yer 'em foin' eawt, loike lots o' married folk,
They allis seem good-tempered like, an' ready wi' a joke.

At number nine th' owd cobbler lives — th' owd chap 'at mends mi shoon,
He's getting very weak an' done, he'll ha' to leov us soon;
He reads his Bible every day, an' sings just loike a lark,
He says he's practisin' for Heaven — he's welly done his wark.

At number ten James Bowton lives — he's th' noicest heawse i' th' row;
He's allis plenty o' sum'at t' eat, an lots o' brass an' o;
An' when he rides an' walks abeawt he's dress'd up very fine,
But he isn't hawve as near to heaven as him at number nine.

At number 'leven mi uncle lives — aw co him uncle Tum,
He goes to concerts, up an' deawn, an' plays a kettle-drum;
I' bands o' music, an' sich things, he seems to tak' a pride,
An' allis makes as big a noise as o i' th' place beside.

At number twelve, an' th' eend o' th' row, Joe Stiggins deals i' ale;
He's sixpenny, an' fourpenny, dark-coloured, an' he's pale;
But aw ne'er touch it, for aw know it's ruined mony a bard —
Awm th' only chap as doesn't drink 'at lives i' Bowton's yard.

An' neaw aw've done aw'll say good-bye, an' leave yo' for awhile;
Aw know aw haven't towd mi tale i' sich a first-rate style;
But iv yo're pleased aw'm satisfied, an' ax for no reward
For tellin' who mi nayburs are 'at live i' Bowton's yard.

ITS HARD TO CEAWER I' TH' CHIMNEY NOOK

IT'S hard to ceawer i' th' chimney nook,
  Fro weary day to day;
An' no kind word, nor lovin' look
  To drive one's care away!
Mi clooas are welly o worn eawt,
  An' neaw aw'm sich a seet,
Aw dunno loike to walk abeawt,
  Unless it's dark at neet.

To get us bread, mi mother sow'd
  Eawr mattresses an' sheets;
An' oh, it is so bitter cowd,
  These frosty, winter neets!
Two ladies kindly co'd one day,
  An' put us deawn some shoon;
They said they'd sheets to give away,
  An' we must ha' some soon.

Eawr Mary Jane's a bonny lass,
  Wi' two such rosy cheeks;
Hoo goes to th' Refuge Sewin' Class,
  An' has done neaw for weeks.
Poor thing! hoo's badly starved, aw know,
  Hoo's scarcely owt to wear;
Aw do so wish 'at somed'y'd co,
  'Ats getten owt to spare.

Her petticoats are o worn eawt;
  Her Sunday frock's i' holes;
An' then her boots — hoo's welly beawt —
  They want booath heels an' soles.
Aw wish mi feyther had a job,
  He looks so strange an' wild;
He'll sit for heawers at th' side o'th' hob,
  An' cry just like a child.

No wonder he should pine an' fret,
   An' look soa discontent;
For th' gas bill isn't settled yet,
   An' th' lon'lord wants his rent.
Mi mother's bin to th' shop to-neet,
   To fetch a bit o' tay;
Hoo says they hardly looken reet,
   Becose hoo conno' pay.

An' who can blame 'em? Nob'dy can;
   They're wur nor us, bi th' mass!
Iv they're to pay for what they han,
   They're loike to ha' some brass;
We'n lived as careful as we con
   Aw'm sure, but after o
A great big shop score's runnin' on,
   For tothry peawned or so.

Aw've etten bacon till aw'm sick;
   Eawr Jimmy has an' o;
An' iv yo'll ax mi uncle Dick,
   He'll tell yo th' same, aw know.
An' porritch aw've had quite anoo,
   For they dunno suit, aw find;
Aw conno' do wi' soup an' stew,
   They fill one full o' wind.

Aw'm glad o' every bit aw get,
   An' rare an' thankful feel;
Aw've allis getten summat yet,
   To mak' misel' a meal.
Thank God, we'n never ax'd i' vain,
   For folk are kind, aw'm sure;
God bless 'em o for what they've gan;
   One conno say no moor.

AW'VE JUST BEEN A-LOOKIN' AT TH' SCHOLARS

AW'VE just been a-lookin' at th' scholars;
    God bless 'em! heaw happy aw feel
To find 'at they'n been so weel done to,
    An' see 'em lookin soa weel.
There's Charley — he's getten new breeches;
    An' Hannah Maria's new shoon;
While owd Billy Wade's youngest dowter,
    Hoo does cut a dash to some tune!

There has been some plannin' an' skeomin',
    There has been some sugarless tay —
An' buttercakes etten beawt butter,
    To get these foine things for to-day!
Neaw, isn't it really surprisin',
    Heaw well th' little childer appear,
When brass is soa hard to get howd of,
    An' wearin' things gettin' soa dear.

If it wurno' for the' kind-hearted women
    (God bless 'em o) helpin' us throo —
While things are soa dreadfully awk'ard —
    'Aw dunna know what we must do.
Iv Mary Ann wants a new bonnet,
    Or Frederick James a new cap,
They'll manage to get 'em a-someheaw,
    They'll oather beg, borrow, or swap.

There's lots o' owd faded silk dresses
    Been used to mack little frocks on;
We've cut an owd cooat o' mi fayther's
    To make up a suit for eawr John.
Aw've seen little Emily Thompson —
    Hoo wur some an' pratty for sure!
There's nob'dy would ever imagine
    Her fayther an' mother are poor.

But foalks have to skeom an' do ole roads,
    An' th' rich abeawt here never dreom,
Heaw one hawve o' th' nayburs abeawt 'em,
    For a bare toarin' on have to skeom.
For, while they've getten so mitch to stur on,
    'At they hardly know what to do wi' 't,
There's mony a poor chilt reawnd abeawt 'em
    Wi' hardly a shoe to its feet.

Eh, aw wish aw wur wealthy, like some foalk,
    An' had summat to spare aw could give,
Aw'd do what this heart-o' moine prompts me,
    Aw'd help thoose abeawt me to live!
Aw'd leeten poor folk o' their burdens,
    Aw'd cheer mony a heart 'at wur sad;
While thoose 'at wur troubled an' deawncast,
    Aw'd try to mak' cheerful an' glad.

Heaw is it 'at foalks are so hampert
    Wi' sich an abundance i' th' lond?
Heaw is it 'at some are i' tatters,
    While others are gaudily donn'd?
Heaw is it 'at some can be livin'
    I' splendour, at foine marble halls,
While others are clemmin' an' starvin',
    Wi' nowt i' their seet but bare walls?

God's good, an' provides us wi' plenty;
    There's mate an' there's clooas for us o,
But these good things — they're hard to get howd on —
    These blessin's 'at ceasin'ly flow —
They seem to be stopp'd on their journey,
    An' laid deawn at th' rich foalks door;
Well, it's happen for th' best 'at it is so;
    God help those 'at's needy an' poor!

CHEER UP, TOILIN' BROTHERS!

CHEER up, toilin' brothers! Cheer up an' be glad;
    There's breeter days for us i' store;
Things are lookin' more sattled i' Lancashire here,
    Neaw' at th' 'Merica war's getten o'er.
Th' long chimnies are smokin' as hard as they con,
    An' th' machinery's wurlin' areawnd;
Owd shopmates 'at havn't bin seen for some years
    Are o gettin' back to th' owd greawnd.

Billy Taylor — he's bin off at Bradford awhile,
    Weavin' woollen for one Mester Hoomes,
But he's brought hissel back to this quarter ogen,
    An' he's peggin' away at th' owd looms.
Their Jack's bin i' Staffordshire one or two years —
    He'rn somewheer tort Bilston, aw think —
He garden'd an' did 'em odd jobs abeawt th' heawse,
    An' he'd twelve bob a week an' his drink.

An owd crony o' mine's bin at Halifax yond,
    Sellin' trotters an' tripe an' ceaw heel;
I' winter he'd cockles an' mussels an' stuff,
    An' he tells me he did rare an' weel.
When th' wayterworks started up tort Swineshaw Brook,
    He wur th' gaffer awhile o'er some men;
But for some cause or other he's left 'em, aw see,
    An' getten i' th' factory ogen.

Polly Breawn's bin i' sarvice for two or three year',
    At a aleheawse o' th' name o' th' Bull's Yead;
An hur an' a waiter there is abeawt th' place,
    They tell'n me, are beawn to be wed.
Eawer Lucy's i' sarvice up Huddersfield way,
    Wi' some chap — aw've forgotten his name;
But, heawever, hoo says hoo shall leave in a month,
    When they'n put her some wark in her frame.

Eh, we han done some knockin' abeawt up an' deawn,
    While trade's bin so bad abeawt here !
We could spin some rare yarns, some on us, aw know —
    We could tell some strange tales, never fear.
We'n had to set to an' do o sorts o' jobs,
    An' we'n bin among o sorts o' folks;
There's theawsands i' Lancashire know what it is,
    To go reawnd o' beggin' wi' pokes.

A lot o' young chaps 'at aw know very weel
    Made it up t' go a-singin' one day,
But th' very furst place 'at they sung at, aw'rn towd,
    They gan 'em a creawn t' go away.
Then they sung for a doctor, a bit further up,
    An' Bolus sent one ov his men
Wi' a shillin' — an' towd 'em he'd give 'em two moor
    Iv they'd sing him "Th' Shurat Song" ogen.

But come, lads, we'll say nowt abeawt this no moor,
    But try an' forget o 'at's past;
It wur th' furst time we'd ever done owt o' this sooart,
    An' we're livin' i' hopes 'at it's th' last.
Let's be careful i' future o'th' bit we can get,
    An' pay off what debts we may owe;
We'n had heawses to live in, clooas, tommy, an' stuff,
    'At's never bin paid for, aw know.

Let's be honest to thoose 'at wur friendly to us,
    An' show bi eawr actions we're men;
There's nob'dy can tell what's before 'em i' th' world —
    We may happen want helpin' ogen.
Neaw yo'll kindly excuse ony blunders aw've made,
    For aw've written as weel as aw con;
An' beg to remain, wi respect an' esteem,
    Yours truly, A Poor Workin' Mon.

MI GRONFEYTHER

AW'VE just had a ramble to th' owd farmheawse,
   Wheer mi gronfeyther lived at so long;
So aw'll draw eawt a bit ov a sketch, which aw hope
   Will noather be tedious nor long.
I' th' furst place, aw feel very sorry to find
   'At th' place isn't same as it wur,
For th' di'mond-shaped windows have o been pood eawt,
   An' they've ta'en th' wooden latch off th' dur.

They've shifted that seot wheer mi gronfeyther sat,
   When at neets he read th' Owd Book:
An' aw couldn't find th' nail wheer he hung up his hat,
   An' th' pot-shelf wur gone eawt o' th' nook.
There's th' dog-kennel yonder, and th' hen-cote aw see,
   An' th' cloos-prop just stonds as it did;
There's a brid-cage hung up wheer mi gronfeyther's wur,
   But aw couldn't see owt ov a brid.

A rare fine owd fellow mi gronfeyther wur,
   Wi' a regular big Roman nose;
An' tho' nearly eighty, he're lusty an' hale,
   An' his cheeks wur as red as a rose.
There wur nowt abeawt him 'at wur shabby or mean;
   As to sense, well, his brain-pon wur full.
He wur allis straightforward i' o 'at he did —
   An owd-fashioned Yorkshur John Bull.

He'd a farm 'at he leased, an' a nice little pond,
   Wheer we used to go fishin' for treawt;
An' aw haven't forgetten when th' hay-time coom reawnd,
   For we childer had mony a blow eawt.
An' when th' "heawsin'" wur done, eh, we had some rare fun,
   Wi' tipplin' an rowlin' on th' stack;
An' then mi owd gronfeyther 'd come wi' his pipe,
   An' carry us abeawt on his back.

When aw wur a lad abeawt thirteen year' owd,
   Aw used to have mony a good ride;
For mi gronfeyther kept a young horse or two then,
   An' a donkey, but th' poor thing died.
He'd a bit ov a garden, at th' backside o' th' heawse,
   Wheer eawr Bobby an' me used to ceawer,
Eatin' goosebris, an' curran's, an' rhubarb, an' crabs;
   In fact, owt wur reet 'at wur seawer.

Neaw, mi gronfeyther, bless him! reet doated o' me;
   An' he'd tell me aw geet a fine lad;
An' he'd mony a time say — as aw've sat on his knee, —
   "Eh, bless thee! tha favours thi dad!"
Then he'd say to mi gronny, "Gie th' lad here some spice,"
   An', whenever hoo happened to bake,
He'd tell her to reach deawn a pot o' presarves,
   An' mak' me a nice presarve cake.

Well, he's long been gone; but a kinder owd mon
   Ne'er existed than Abram wur!
Th' last time aw wur o'er theer, an' saw him alive,
   He wur sittin' eawtside his dur.
He geet howd o' mi hond when we parted that day,
   An' aw think aw shall never forget
Heaw he looked i' mi face when aw're goin' away:
   It wur th' last time 'at ever we met!

A week or two after th' owd fellow 'd a stroke;
   An' fell off his cheer on to th' floor;
They lifted him up, an' they took him to bed,
   But he never wur gradely no moor.
Good-bye, dear owd gronfeyther! nob'dy i' th' world
   Could be fonder than aw wur o' thee;
An', if in th' future dear bonds are renewed,
   Tha'rt one 'at aw'm hopin' to see!

MI GRONNY

HOO'S turned eighty-one — mi gronny is neaw,
   An' yet for her age hoo's reet clever;
An' her silvery locks spread abeawt o'er her broo
   Macks her look just as bonny as ever.
Aw wur theer t' other neet, an' aw thowt to misel'
   God bless her! hoo's farantly lookin'!
An' it wur a grand seet, as wi' tears in her een,
   Hoo sat readin' her Bible an' smookin'.

Hoo wur browt up i' Yorkshur, 'mong fields an' fleawers,
   An' drank wayter pure fro' th' spring;
An' hoo loved to get up when th' sun geet up,
   An' hearken th' cuckoo sing.
Th' owd foalk had a farm, an' they'd lots o' milk,
   An' hoo geet it warm fro' th' ceaw;
An' it did her good, an' nourished her blood,
   Or hoo metn't ha' lived till neaw.

Hoo's a widow, an' has been for th' last forty year,
   Soa hoo hasn't a bad husband to bother;
Hoo's a dowter 'at hasn't said "I will" yet,
   An' hoo tarries awhoam wi' her mother.
Neaw this dowter an' hur they baken an' done,
   An' sell potates, boath English an' foreign;
An' other odd matters i' th' grocery loine,
   Sich as sceawerin'-stones, candles, an' herrin'.

Neaw, mi Gronny's a Christian, aw'd ha' yo' to know,
   Says her prayers at th' bed-soide every neet;
Gies her customers measure an' weight for their brass,
   An' as fur as hoo knows hoo does reet.
Soa God bless mi owd Gronny, God bless her, say I;
   May that heart o' hur's never grow cowd
Till hoo's baked ole her fleawr up and sowd ole her bread,
   An' getten a hundred year owd!

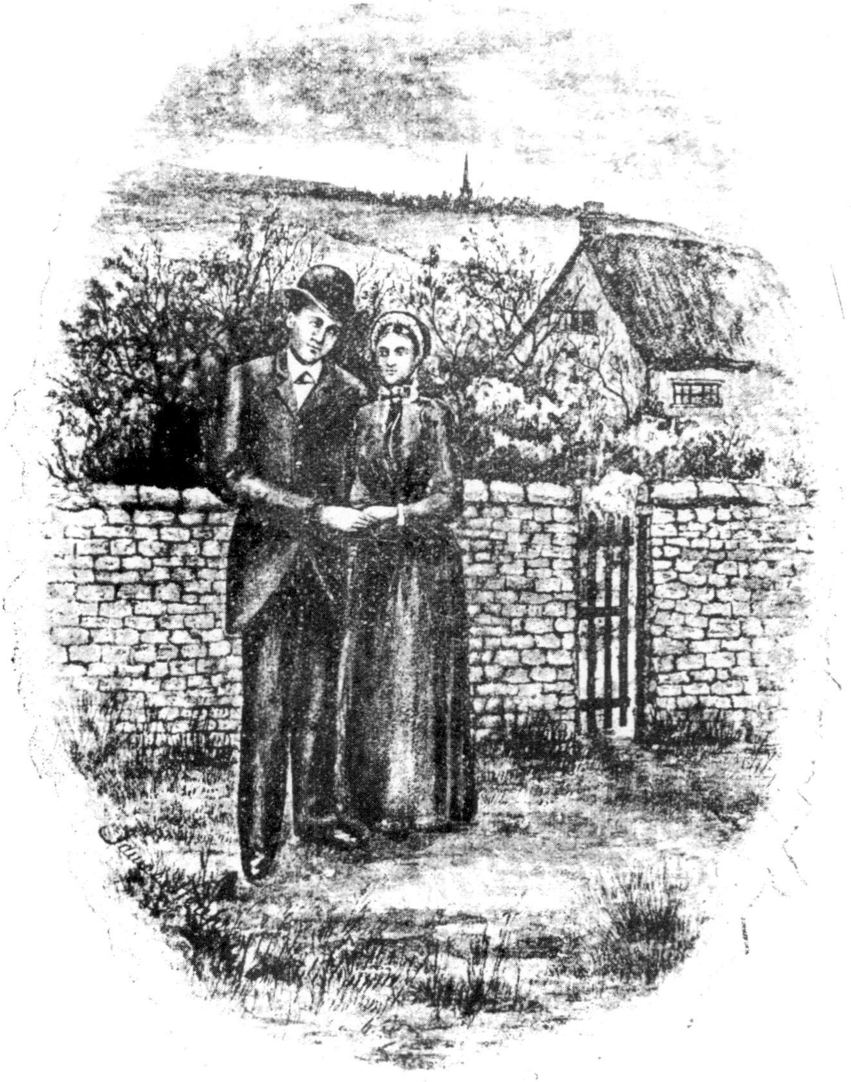

MALLY AN' JONAS

COME, Mally, owd woman, it's near forty year,
   Sin' thee an' me furst coom together;
We've had mony a breet smile, ah, an' mony a sad tear,
   An' experienced booath good an' bad weather.
As eawr 'Lizabeth's gone to look after thi geawn,
   An' eawr Tum's rubbin' th' mare deawn i' th' stable,
What thinks ta, owd lass, iv we sitten us deawn,
   An' have a nice chat while we're able?

Owd age is fast whitenin' eawr yeads one con see;
   An' these shanks o' eawrs are no' so nimble
As they wur when aw held thee th' furst time on mi knee,
   An' tha rapp'd me o'er th' yead wi' thi thimble.
I' fancy aw often look back to thoose days,
   When tha lived wi' thi aunt i' th' Flag Alley;
There wur nob'dy aw'm sure had a prattier face,
   An' aw did think some weel on thee, Mally!

Aw bowt thee some ear-rings o' reet solid gowd,
   An' some side-combs to stick i' thi hair;
An' when we walked eawt, aw wur lots o' times towd,
   Tha wur th' han'somest lass i' o th' fair.
True, sin then a great deol o' thi charms have gone dead,
   An' tha'rt nowt near as lusty an' clever;
But, spite o' thi wrinkles an' silvery yead,
   Aw love thee as dearly as ever.

There's one thing aw've noticed owd lass, an' it's this, —
   That whenever tha's had ony trouble,
An' tha's come an' pretended to borrow a kiss,
   Tha allis would pay me back double.
Neaw, when ta'en an' compared wi' a woman like thee,
   What's beauty, position, or riches!
But tha seems to be shapin' for cryin' aw see,
   So get on wi' mendin' mi britches.

"Neaw, drop it, do, Jonas, tha's said quite enuff;
   Mon, tha'rt worse than tha wur when we're courtin';
An' at that time tha turned eawt a lot o' queer stuff,
   'At needed some weedin' an' sortin'.
Aw'm surprised at a grey-yeaded fellow like thee;
   Still, it's nobbut thi fun 'at tha'rt pokin';
An', someheaw, tha never con let me a-be
   When tha'rt ceawrin' i' th' corner an' smokin'.

Aw see 'at there's one o' thi waist-buttons gone,
   An' one o' thi gallowses brocken;
Tha needn't ha' gone abeawt this way mon,
   If tha'd oppen'd thi meawth an' just spocken.
Aw'm expectin' eawr 'Lizabeth here very soon;
   An' eawr Will's abeawt leavin' Jane Tupper;
If tha'll push a few lumps o' dry wood under th' oon,
   Aw'll see abeawt mackin' some supper.

As it's Setterday neet, we shall want summat nice;
   Heaw would t' relish some tripe or some trotters?
As tha knows, lad, we've had some good stuff once or twice
   At that shop th' next but one to owd Potter's.
If tripe doesn't suit thee when goin' to bed
   Aw con mak thee a mess o' good porritch;
We've some capital meal 'at owd Carrier Ned
   Browt wi' him fro' Gregson's at Nor'itch.

But tha musn't forget tha's to wesh thee a bit,
   An' go deawn to th' shop for some stuff;
We want a few beons, an' some corn for th' owd tit,
   An' tha wants some 'bacco an' snuff.
It's Sunday to-morn! Oh aw like it to come,
   For it's th' best day we have i' ole th' seven, —
A day when one's soul con look on tow'rds whoam,
   An', on earth, get a foretaste o' heaven!"

AW'VE TURNED MI BIT O'GARDEN O'ER

AW'VE turned mi bit o' garden o'er,
　An' set mi seed an' o;
Soa neaw aw've done aw'll rest a bit,
　An' sit an' watch it grow.
It's noice to have a little spot,
　Where one can ceawer 'em deawn,
A quiet, comfortable place,
　Eawtside o' th' busy teawn,
Where one can sit an' smoke their poipe,
　An' have a friendly chat,
Or read th' newspapper o'er a bit,
　Or talk abeawt Shurat;
Or listen to some owd man's tale,
　Some vet'ran come fro' th' wars;
Aw loike to yer 'em spin their yarn,
　An' show their wounds an' scars.

One neet aw thowt aw'd tak' a walk
　As far as th' Hunter's Teawer,
To beg a daisy root or two:
　Tom's gan me mony a fleawer.
They're bloomin' i' mi garden neaw,
　Aw've sich a bonny show;
Aw've daisies, pinks, carnations, too,
　An' pollyants an' o.
Yo' couldn't think heaw preawd aw feel,
　O' every plant an' fleawer;
Aw couldn't ha' cared for childer moor —
　Aw've nursed 'em mony a heawer.
But tho' they neaw look fresh an' fair,
　They'll droop their yeds an' dee;
They hanno' long to tarry here —
　They're just loike yo' an' me.

Dark-lookin' cleawds are gatherin' reawnd,
　　Aw think it's beawn to rain;
There's nowt could pleos me better neaw,
　　Aw should be rare an' fain!
Mi bit o' seed wants deggin' o'er,
　　To help to mak' it spreawt;
It's summat loike a choild's first teeth,
　　'At wanten helpin' eawt.
But aw'll be off, afore aw'm wet,
　　It's getten reet agate;
An' while it comes aw think aw'll get
　　A bit o' summat t' eat;
For oh! it is a hungry job,
　　This workin' eawt o' th' door;
Th' committee should alleaw for this,
　　An' give one rayther moor.

Aw should so loike a good blow eawt,
　　A feed off beefsteak pie;
But aw can ne'er get nowt loike that
　　Wi' th' bit aw draw, not I!
Aw'm glad enough o' porritch neaw,
　　Or tothrey cowd potates;
If aw can get enoo o' these,
　　Aw'st do till th' factory gates.
It's welly gan o'er rainin', so
　　Aw'll have another look,
An' see heaw th' garden's gettin' on;
　　An' then aw'll get a book,
An read an heawer or two for th' woife,
　　An' sing a bit for Ted;
Then poo mi clogs off, fasten th' doors,
　　An' walk up steers to bed.

ODE TO TH' SUN

HAIL, owd friend ! aw'm fain to see thee:
  Wheer has t' been so mony days?
Lots o' times aw've looked up for thee,
  Wishin' aw could see thi face.
Th' little childer reawned abeawt here,
  Say they wonder wheer tha'rt gone;
An' they wanten me to ax thee
  T' show thisel' as oft as t' con.

Come an' see us every mornin';
  Come, these droopin' spirits cheer:
Peep thro' every cottage window;
  Tha'll be welcome everywheer.
Show thisel i' o thi splendour;
  Throw that gloomy veil aside;
What dost t' creep to th' back o'th' cleawds for?
  Tha's no fau'ts nor nowt to hide.

Flashy clooas an' bits o foinery
  Help to mend sich loike as me:
Veils improve some women's faces,
  But, owd friend, they'll noan mend thee.
Things deawn here 'at we co'n pratty
  Soon begin to spoil an' fade;
But tha still keeps up thi polish,
  Tha'rt as breet as when new made.

Tha wur theer when th' hosts o' heaven
  Sweetly sang their mornin' song;
But tha looks as young as ever,
  Tho' tha's bin up theer so long.
An' for ages tha's bin shinin' —
  Smilin' o' this world o' eawrs;
Blessin' everythin' tha looks on,
  Makin' th' fruit grow — oppenin' fleawers.

It wur thee 'at Adam looked on,
   When i' th' garden bi hisel';
An' tha smoiled upon his labour —
   Happen helped him — who can tell?
It wur thee 'at Joshua spoke to
   On his way to th' promised land;
When, as th' good owd Bible tells us,
   Theaw obeyed his strange command.

Tha'll ha' seen some curious antics
   Played deawn here bi th' human race;
Some tha couldn't bear to look on,
   For tha shawmed an' hid thi face.
Mony a toime aw see thee blushin',
   When tha'art leavin' us at neet:
An' no wonder, for tha's noticed
   Things we'n done 'at's noan been reet.

After o tha comes to own us,
   Tho' we do so mich 'at's wrong;
Even neaw tha'rt shinin' breetly,
   Helpin' me to write this song.
Heaw refreshin'! Heaw revivin'!
   Stay as long as ever t' con;
We shall noan feel hawve as happy,
   Hawve as leetsome, when tha'rt gone.

Oh! For th' sake o' foalk 'at's poorly,
   Come an' cheer us wi thi rays;
We forgetten 'at we ail owt
   When we see thy dear owd face.
Every mornin' when it's gloomy
   Lots o' foalk are seen abeawt;
Some at th' door-steps, some at th' windows,
   Watchin' for thee peepin' eawt.

ROWL AWAY, THEAW GRAND OWD OCEAN

ROWL away, theaw grand owd ocean,
   Dash thi spray on th' pebbly shore;
Like some giant i' devotion,
   Singin' praises evermore.
Talk o' true an' earnest worship!
   Great revivals! dear-a-me!
Why, there isn't a sect i' th' nation
   'At con hawve come up to thee.

Baptists, Independents, Quakers,
   Followers o' Young an' Joe;
Ranters, Unitarians, Shakers,
   These are nowt — tha dreawns 'em o.
Organ, singers, parson, people,
   Let these mak' what noise they will;
Ring o' th' bells they han i' th' steeple,
   Tha poipes eawt aboon 'em still.

Oh, aw loike to yer thee roarin';
   Loike thee when i' gradely trim;
When wi' mighty voice tha'rt pourin'
   Eawt some grand thanksgivin' hymn!
Priests han mumbled, people muttered,
   What's bin looked upon as foine;
Still their praises are no uttered
   Hawve so heartily as thoine.

O, heaw charmin' 'tis at midneet!
   Heaven's breet lamps lit up aboon;
Thee deawn here, like some vast mirror,
   Silvered o'er wi' th' leet o' th' moon!
What are these 'at look like childer,
   Bi their mother gently led?
Th' moon's browt th' stars to have a bathe here,
   Just before they're put to bed!

Th' sun may shed his brilliant lustre;
    Th' moon display her queenly peawer;
Th' bonny twinklin' stars may muster
    All their force at th' midneet heawer.
Th' woind may roar i' wild commotion,
    Or may blow a gentle breeze:
Still, ah, still owd briny ocean,
    Theaw can charm me moor nor these.

Oh, aw loike to yer thy music,
    Moor nor th' bells 'at sweetly chime;
For thy voice is ever seawndin'
    Grandly solemn an' sublime!
Eawr poor efforts, tho' inferior,
    Very often have t' be bowt;
But, tho' thine's so much superior,
    Tha ne'er thinks o' chargin' owt.

When God's people fled fro' bondage,
    Tramp'd thro' th' wilderness so long;
An' fair Miriam played on th' timbrel,
    Did ta help 'em i' their song?
When preawd Pharaoh's host o'ertook 'em,
    An' th' poor things i' terror stood;
Do we read 'at theaw forsook 'em?
    Nay, but helped 'em o tha could.

Londin' here fro' th' great Atlantic,
    Sometoimes tha does use us bad;
Foamin', ravin', fairly frantic;
    Tossin' ships abeawt loike mad!
Other toimes tha's bin quite different,
    Noather awkward, cross, nor nowt;
Same as if tha'd bin asleep theer,
    Just as calm an' still as owt.

Oh, we connot blame thee, ocean;
   Often toimes we've yerd it said,
'At tha uses th' gentlest motion,
   When tha'rt movin' nearest th' dead.
Whoile a mon's o reet an' hearty,
   He may foind thee rayther ruff;
Iv he lies theer deod an' helpless
   Then, owd friend, tha'rt kind enuff.

Foalk 'at feel there's summat wantin';
   Drinkers deep o' sorrow's cup;
These should yer thi merry chantin',
   Bless us tha'd soon cheer 'em up!
Oh, an' tha'rt a kind physician;
   Well it is tha wants no fee;
Weakly folk i' my condition
   Couldn't pay, they'd ha' to dee.

Mony a toime aw've sit deawn, sadly
   Broodin' o'er mi load o' woe,
Feelin' gradely sick an' badly,
   Crush'd wi' cares 'at few can know.
O at once these cares han vanished;
   Not a fear left, not a deawt;
Every gloomy thowt's bin banished,
   When aw've yeard thee poipin' eawt.

Foalk 'at live i' teawns an' cities,
   Conno yer thee same as me;
Oh! but it's a theawsand pities!
   Everyone should hearken thee.
Rowl away, then, grand owd ocean;
   Dash thi spray on th' pebbly shore;
Tha ne'er flags i' thy devotion —
   Allis singin' — evermore.

BISPHAM

BISPHAM here pratty?
Aw think it *is* pratty;
Foind me another spot
Lookin' soa "natty".
Hedgerows are bloomin',
Ole the village perfumin',
An' garden beds put on their pleasantest looks.
Th' good childer's new weshed, love,
An' th' bad ones new threshed, love,
While th' dullards are kept to their slates an' their books.

Bispham here pratty?
Why, bless thi loife, Matty,
Thee on wi' thi bonnet
An' come here to-neet;
Throstles are singin',
An' th' village bells ringin',
An' daisies are growin' reet under one's feet.
Fling away sadness, love,
Frettin' is madness, love;
Come thi ways here an' tha'll see a grand seet!

An' deawn on thi shanks, lass,
Return God thi thanks, lass;
We've never deserved
These dainties 'at's served.
Why, look up aboon,
At th' breet queenly moon,
Heaw grandly hoo pours deawn her silvery leet!
Look at th' stars creawdin' near,
Loike childer gone theer
To see their dear mother, an' bid her good neet.

Bispham here pratty?
Aw think it *is* pratty;
Then come thi ways, Matty,
An' see for thisel;
Come while it's May, love,
For th' fleawers fade away, love,
An' th' east winds may silence ole th' songsters i' th' dell.
Aw've tidied mi garden walks,
Shifted th' owd beon stalks,
An' dusted mi parlour, expectin' tha'd come.
Soa if tha's a bonnet, lass,
Look sharp an' don it, lass.
An' visit th' owd bard in his countryfied whoam.

WHAT! ANOTHER CRACKED POET!

WHAT! Another cracked poet! Bi thi mass, Jim, owd lad,
    Aw thowt we'd enoo o' this mack;
An' iv tha'll alleaw me to say what aw think,
    Tha desarves a good stick to thi back.
Aw'll tell thee what, lad, tha'll be awfully clemmed
    Iv tha'rt thinkin' to live bi thi pen.
Iv tha wants to get on, get some porritch an' milk,
    An' some good cheese an' bread neaw an' then.

Neaw, aw've had some experience i' this mak' o' wark;
    Aw've bin thirty odd year i' this schoo';
An' what have aw managed to larn does ta think?
    Well, aw've managed to larn awm a foo'!
Tha'll find 'at this scribblin's a very poor trade,
    An' tha'd ger along better bi th' hawve,
Iv tha'd start as a quack, wi' a tapeworm or two,
    Or a few decent pills an' some sawve.

Ive tha still feels determined to turn eawt as bard,
    Aw'd advise thee to let nob'dy know,
Or tha'll rue it to th' very last day 'at tha lives,
    Tha'll wish tha'd kept quiet — tha will so!
Iv Betty o' Bowsers at th' bottom o' th' lone
    Happens t' lose an' owd favourite cat,
Very loikely th' furst body tha chances to meet
    Will ax thee to write abeawt that.

Iv a couple gets wed, or a chap licks his wife,
    Or some scamp in a train steals a kiss,
Aw'll warrant th' furst gossip tha meets 'll say, "Jim,
    Tha'll spin us a rhyme abeawt this".
Tha'll be loikely to feel a bit flattered at first,
    An' think it a stunnin' good trade;
But let me impress just one fact on thi mind,
    It's this, Jim, tha'll never get paid.

Iv tha's ony opinions 'at doesn't just square
    Wi' thoose 'at are held bi thi friends,
They'll look on thee coolly, as iv tha'rn a thief,
    An' turn thee adrift till tha mends.
Iv tha knows heaw to flatter, an' wink at men's wrongs,
    Tha may manage t' get on very weel;
But, tackle their habits, expose their mean tricks,
    An' they'll shun thee as iv tha'rn the de'il!

Well, aw've towd thee mi moind, tha can do what tha loikes,
    Go on rhymin', or let it alone;
Iv th' latter — thi friends may provide thee a fish;
    Iv th' former — they'll give thee a stone.
An' what abeawt sellin' thi poetry, Jim?
    Neaw, tha'll foind that a job aw can tell;
Iv tha'rt treated loike other poor Lancashire bards,
    Tha'll ha' to go sell 'em thisel'!

Heaw would t' loike goin' reawnd wi' a bag full o' books?
    Heaw would t' loike to go hawkin' thi brains?
Or, when tha's bin tryin' to do some kind act,
    To be towd tha'rt a foo' for thi pains.
Aw can tell thee this, Jim, it's aboon twenty year',
    Sin' aw wur set deawn as a foo';
An', tho' it's a charge at once doesn't loike to own,
    Awm beginnin' to think 'at it's true.

Thee stick to recitin' — tha'rt clever at that;
    In fact, there's few loike thee i' th' lond,
An' booath i' th' pathetic an' th' humorous vein
    Tha'rt reckoned a very good hond.
But aw'll drop it, owd friend, for aw'm gradely fag'd eawt;
    Booath mi brain an' mi hand 'gin to tire;
Iv tha loikes tha can stick these few lines i' thi book;
    Or — iv tha prefers it — i' th' fire.

"ONLY A POET"

"Only a poet", a schemer o' schemes;
A weaver o' fancies, a dreamer o' dreams;
Insanely eccentric, wi' long flowin' hair,
An' eyes strangely bright, wi' a meanin'less stare!
"Only a poet" — that's all, nowt no moor;
An', as every one knows, often needy an' poor;
Tho' that little fault may be remedied soon,
If th' minstrel could allis get paid for his tune.
Then look what a lot their strange yarns often cost!
Just fancy five sov'rins for "Paradise Lost"!
Why, for much less than that, there are theawsands o' men
Who would not only *lose* it, but *find* it ogen!

Neaw supposin' yo' bowt some good clooas to yo'r back,
Some beef-steaks an' onions, or owt o' that mak';
These would bring yo' some comfort, an' help yo' to live,
But yo'll dee if yo'n nowt but what poets con give.
"Only a poet" — a gazer at th' moon,
Or soarin' aloft i' some mental balloon;
Ah, some of 'em wingin' their flight to God's throne,
An' seemin' t' forget they'n a whoam o' their own,
Wheer a wife may be ceaw'red in an owd tattered geawn,
Very patiently waitin' till th' husband comes deawn.
"Only a poet", a spinner o' rhymes,
An' never caught worshippin' "dollars an' dimes".

"Only a poet" — a star-gazin' bard
'At met tell yo' th' earth's distance fro' th' sun to a yard;
But question him closely on trade, or bank shares,
An' he'll soon show his ignorance bi th' way 'at he stares.
Wanderin' throo' country lanes all the day long,
Gabblin' strange jargon, or croonin' some song;
Pennin' grand thowts 'at may mak' a world stare,
Then die in a mad-heawse, like poor John Clare!
"Only a poet" — ah! but what does that mean?
Bein' passed bi a naybur witheawt bein' seen;
Becose just across there comes Alderman Stott,
An' he gets th' warm greetin' th' poor bard should ha' got!
"Only a poet" — he's nowt he con spare;
If his feelin's *are* hurt a bit, what need yo' care?

For a poet is noan a much use as a friend,
Since he's nowt he con give one, nor nowt he con lend.
"Only a poet", so let him alone,
Or, if yo' think fit, yo' may fling him a bone;
He lives o' sich stuff — bones an' owd meawldy books,
At least one would think soa, to judge by his looks.
Yo' keep eawt o' th' way on him, foalks, for he's sure
To speak abeawt summat yo'n ne'er yeard befoor;
He's likely to tell yo' yo'n brains i' yo'r yead.
An' a soul that'll live when yo'r body's gone dead;
He'll talk about spirit friends hoverin' areawnd,
When yo' know they're asleep, fast asleep, deawn i'th' greawnd.

He'll offer to lead yo' through nature's sweet beawers,
An' bid yo' admire her grand fruitage an' fleawers.
Very grand an' poetical; nice food for kings,
Or bein's 'at flutter abeawt us wi' wings;
But one couldn't weel offer to clothe a bare back,
Or feed hungry bellies wi' stuff o' that mak'.
"Only a poet", like Bloomfield or Burns,
'At may happen amuse yo' an' vex yo' i' turns;
Neaw charmin' his readers wi' th' thowts fro' his pen,
Thus winnin' their heartiest plaudits, an' then,
It may be th' next minute yo'r filled wi disgust
At some sarcastic hit, or some pointed home-thrust!

"*Only* a poet"! What moor do yo' want?
Some narrow-souled parson to rave an' to rant
Abeawt th' heat an' th' dimensions, an' th' people i' hell,
Till yo' fancy 'at th' chap must ha' bin' theer hissel.
Yet there are foalk i' th' world 'at don't think it amiss
To pay hundreds a year for sich twaddle as this;
While others, entitled to love an' respect,
Are treated too often wi' scorn an' neglect!
"*Only a Poet*", what moor do yo' crave,
To sweeten life's journey fro' th' cradle to th' grave?
Which is th' likeliest — think yo' — to help us along, —
An owd musty creed, or a good hearty song?

TO A CRICKET

SING on, there's nobbut thee an' me;
We'll mack th' heawse ring, or else we'll see.
Thee sing thoose little songs o' thine,
As weel as t' con, an' aw'll sing mine.
We'll have a concert here to-neet,
Soa pipe thi notes eawt clear an' sweet:
Thee sing a stave or two for me,
An' then aw'll sing a bit for thee.
That's reet, goa on, mi little guest,
Theaw tries to do thi very best,
An' aw'll do th' same, then thee an' me
May get eawr names up yet tha'll see.
Why, th' childer's listenin' neaw at th' door;
There's creawds abeawt! There is, forshure.
Heaw pleosed they seem — dear little things!
Aw'd sooner sing for them than kings.